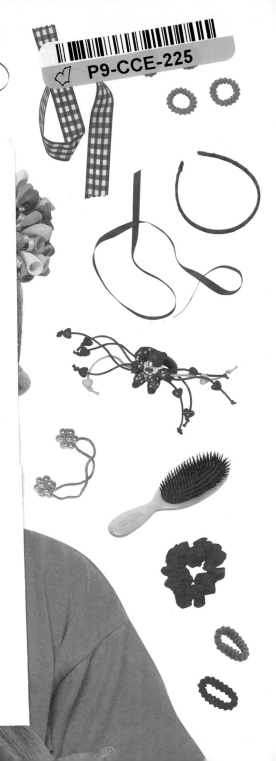

# BRILLIANT BRAIDS, BEADS & BOWS

## 25 fantastic hairstyles that you can create yourself!

Jacki Wadeson

ARMADILLO

This edition is published by Armadillo, an imprint of Anness Publishing Ltd,
Blaby Road, Wigston, Leicestershire LE18 4SE; info@anness.com; www.annesspublishing.com

If you like the images in this book and would like to investigate using them for publishing, promotions
or advertising, please visit our website www.practicalpictures.com for more information.

Publisher: Joanna Lorenz
Senior Editor: Caroline Beattie
Editors: Sue Grabham and Richard McGinlay
Photographer: John Freeman

Hair Stylist: Debbi Finlow
Designers: Tony Sambrook
and Edward Kinsey
Production Controller: Mai-Ling Collyer

PUBLISHER'S NOTE

Manufacturer: Anness Publishing Ltd, Blaby Road, Wigston, Leicestershire LE18 4SE, England
For Product Tracking go to: www.annesspublishing.com/tracking
Batch: 0232-22463-1127

# Introduction

Doing your hair is such fun, and you'll be surprised to see how easy it is to create different styles. There are lots of things you can do, whether your hair is straight, wavy or curly. All you need is a brush and comb, and as many bright ribbons, beads, bows, covered bands and flowers as you can lay your hands on. Ask a grown-up if you can raid their sewing box – you'll find lots of interesting things in there that you can use. Learn how to do a simple braid (also known as a plait) and ponytail first, as these form the basis of many styles. It's great if you have a friend to help you, and then you can do each other's hair. Mix and match your styles and accessories to go with whatever you are wearing. You can jazz up a plain T-shirt or give an outfit a whole new look just by changing your hair.

Happy braiding!

Jacki Wadeson

# Contents

# Simple Braid

This three-stranded style is a lot easier than it looks.

**1** Part your hair from the middle front to the nape of your neck. Divide one half of your hair into three equal sections and hold the outer sections with your hands.

**2** Cross the back section over the middle section. Use your fingers to make sure that the other two sections remain separate.

**3** Now cross the front section over the middle section. It is important to pull all three strands of hair evenly as you work, so that your braid is straight.

**5** Hold the end of your braid about 5cm/2in from the end. Take a covered band and slip it over the end, then twist it back over as many times as you need to, so as to keep the braid secure.

**4** Now you can see how the braid is beginning to form. Carry on braiding, crossing the sections, right over middle and left over middle.

6

# Perfect Ponytail

1 Brush your hair straight back using long sweeping strokes to make sure there are no knots. Tease any knots out by brushing gently from the bottom.

2 Place a fabric-covered band on your wrist, then pull your hair together with your hands at the back of your head.

3 Slip the band off your wrist and over the ponytail. Hold your hair in one hand and twist the band with the other.

4 Thread the ponytail through the band again (your hands will swap positions) and repeat.

A ponytail is one of the easiest styles to do. It keeps hair tidy and stops it getting into a tangle.

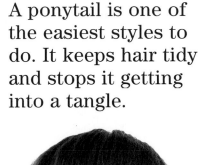

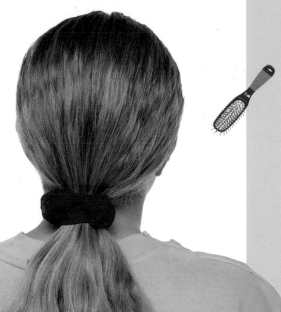

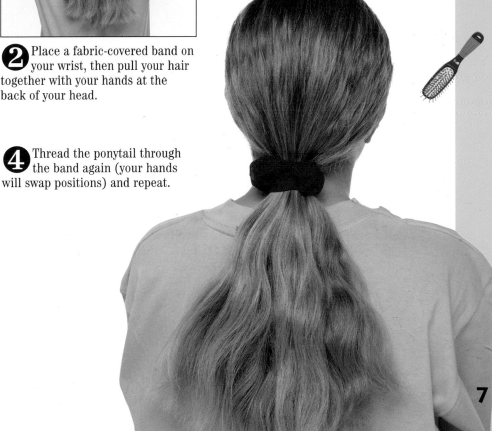

7

# Twist and Roll

A really simple style that can be done in a jiffy, using a long fabric-covered band and a few twists of your wrists.

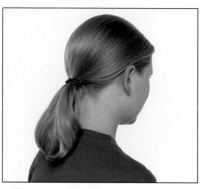

**1** Brush your hair into a ponytail at the nape of your neck (see page 7). Secure in a covered band.

**2** Take a long fabric-covered band and place it under your ponytail. Cross over the ends over the top and hold them in your hands.

**3** Twist the fabric band around the ponytail, right down the length of your hair, until you reach the ends of your hair.

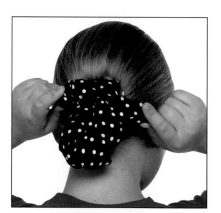

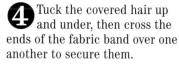

**4** Tuck the covered hair up and under, then cross the ends of the fabric band over one another to secure them.

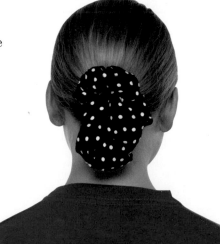

# Do the Flip

A nifty way to wear your ponytail – you just need a styler to flip it up and thread it down.

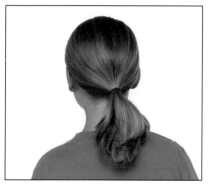

**1** Brush your hair straight back and secure at the nape of your neck in a covered band.

**2** Gently push the straight end of the styler down the middle of the back of your head, behind the covered band.

**3** Hold the straight end of the styler and thread your ponytail through the loop, then pull the styler down and your hair will flip through.

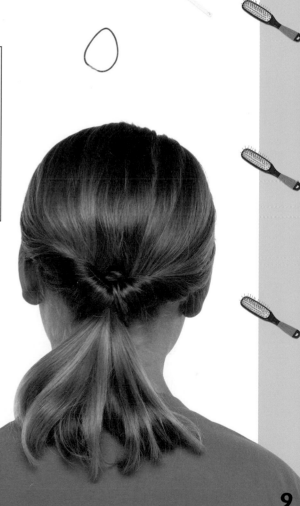

9

# Beading

Add bright beads – as many as you like – to liven up your hair.

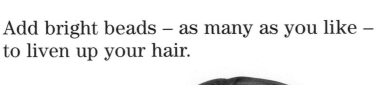

**1** Following the basic instructions given on page 6, braid a small piece of hair down one side of your face. Hold the ends together with a grip, then take a single bead and a small piece of glittery thread that you have folded to form a loop.

**2** Pass the looped end of the thread through the middle of the bead. This is easiest if you make sure that the beads you use have quite large holes in the middle.

**3** Remove the grip from the end of the braid and pass that through the loop of thread. Make sure you keep a firm hold on the bead, so it doesn't fall off.

**4** Push the bead towards the braid, then pull the ends of the thread; the end of your braid will pull through the middle of the bead. Continue pulling until the end of the braid comes through the bead.

**5** Wrap the thread around and around the end of your braid, making sure that the strands lie flat. Carry on until you have covered about 1cm/½in of hair below the bead.

**6** Cross over the ends of the thread, then repeat to form a knot. If necessary, cut the ends of the thread off, being careful not to snip the end of your braid.

**TIP**
*Make sure you always keep your hair beads in a safe place away from babies or small children, who may think they are confectionery.*

# Accessories

Clips, hairbands and floppy bows change your look in an instant.

**2** Smooth your hair back and secure it with a zigzag band which fastens at the back of your neck underneath your hair.

**3** Take the front section of your hair and clasp it in a band which has been decorated with short pieces of ribbon.

**1** Scoop your hair up into a ponytail on top of your head and secure it in a band.

**4** Scoop the front hair back from the ears to the crown and clip on a chiffon bow.

**5** Add a neat velvet-covered band to dress up a low ponytail.

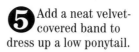

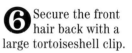

**6** Secure the front hair back with a large tortoiseshell clip.

**9** Fine ribbon bows make tiny braids look extra special.

**7** Hairbands come in all shapes and sizes and simply slide into place.

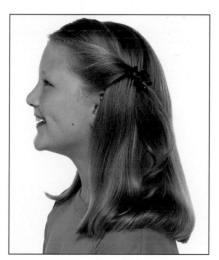

**8** Take a small section of hair, twist it up and over and secure it in a mini clip.

**13**

# Bouncy Bunches

Any length of hair can be scooped up into pretty bunches. Add bright ribbons in fun shades for every day and fairy bows for party time.

**TIP**
*Gift-wrap ribbon is ideal for making bows and covering grips.*

**1** Part your hair in the middle from front to back. Put a covered band over one hand, so that it sits on your knuckles (this makes it easy to slip over your bunch) and hold one half of your hair in the other hand.

**2** Slip the bunch right the way through the covered band, holding your hair tightly with one hand and using your thumb to pull the band tight.

**3** Twist the covered band around once, then put your fingers through the loop and pull the bunch through. Do this again until the band is tight enough to hold your hair.

**4** Take a short piece of ribbon and tie it around the bunch, then make a bow. Repeat for the other side.

**5** For fairy bows, twist thin ribbon around the top half of a grip, starting at the open end. Tie a tiny bow at the end of each grip. Use lots of different shades and simply push the grips into place around your hairline.

# Heidi Hi

**1** Part your hair in the middle from front to back. Comb half over one shoulder and divide into three equal pieces. Then braid right down to the ends of the hair.

**2** Push a small stretch band over one hand so that it sits on your knuckles, while holding the end of the braid in the other hand. Don't let go or your braid will unravel.

**3** Comb the other half of your hair over to the front of your shoulder and braid in the same way. Try to keep the braids even by pulling equally on each section of hair.

**4** Secure the end of the braid in a stretch band, as before, twisting it back to make sure it is tight enough to hold your braid.

**5** You can either leave your braids down or pin them on top of your head with a novelty slide.

Once you have learned how to braid your hair, you can ring the changes using different types of bands or looping the braids over your head.

**TIP**

*Use a comb to the perfect the art of getting your parting straight. Your hairstyle looks even better if your parting doesn't wiggle around like a snake!*

17

# Topsy Turvy

A topknot is great if you are
growing out your fringe
because you can rein
in all those little ends
that tend to stick out.

**TIP**
*You can twist ribbons
together for a really
unusual hairband.
Choose shades that
match your clothes.*

18

1 Brush your hair through to make sure you haven't got any tangles. Use the thumb of each hand to divide off the top section of the hair from your ears up to the top of your head.

2 Push a fabric-covered band over the fingers of one hand so that it rests on your knuckles, and clasp the topknot of hair in your other hand.

3 Slip a band over the hair and twist it, ready to repeat. Be careful not to let go of the topknot while you are twisting the band around your topknot.

4 Twist the band around again in exactly the same way. If it feels a little bit loose, then twist again until the topknot feels nice and firm. The number of times you need to twist depends on how big your band is.

5 You can dress up your topknot by taking two lengths of thin ribbon in different shades and placing them around your head like a hairband. Simply tie the ends at the back of your neck, under your hair, where no one can see.

# French Fancy

Straight bob-length hair looks great with small braids when they are cleverly twisted to give a trendy teen style. An unusual hair slide (we found a beautiful pair of elephants) adds the perfect finish.

**1** Part off a small band of hair on the top of your head. Lift the front of this section and start braiding. As you cross the strands, bring a little more hair into the outer strands and work it into the braid.

**TIP**
*You can decorate plain slides by sticking pictures or buttons on them.*

**2** Take a small section of hair at the side of your head, in front of your ear, and braid from the roots to the ends. When you reach the ends, secure in a covered band.

**3** Take another small section of hair at the other side of your head in front of your ear and braid in the same way, until you reach the ends. Secure in a covered band.

**4** Take the two side braids and lift them onto the top of your head. Secure these, and the end of your top braid, in a large slide which will cover all the ends.

**5** For a quick change, tie the ends of the braids in a fabric-covered band and divide the back hair into two neat little bunches with matching fabric-covered bands.

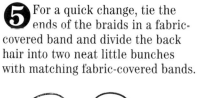

21

# Beaded Braids

**1** Part your hair in the middle, then take a small section of hair and divide into three equal strands. Begin to braid, working down from the roots to the ends. See page 6 for full directions.

**2** Slip the beads over the end of the braid, as shown on pages 10–11. Attach a second bead in the same way and bind the ends with thread so the beads don't fall off.

**3** Make as many more braids as you would like; we did three on each side. Make sure that you put the beads on at the same level on all the braids.

**4** Brush the loose hair up high on the crown of your head and secure with a fabric-covered band. Brush the ponytail through so it's nice and smooth.

Tiny braids with beads threaded through the ends look difficult to do but are so easy. Bead just a few braids around your face or ask a friend to help you do them all over your head.

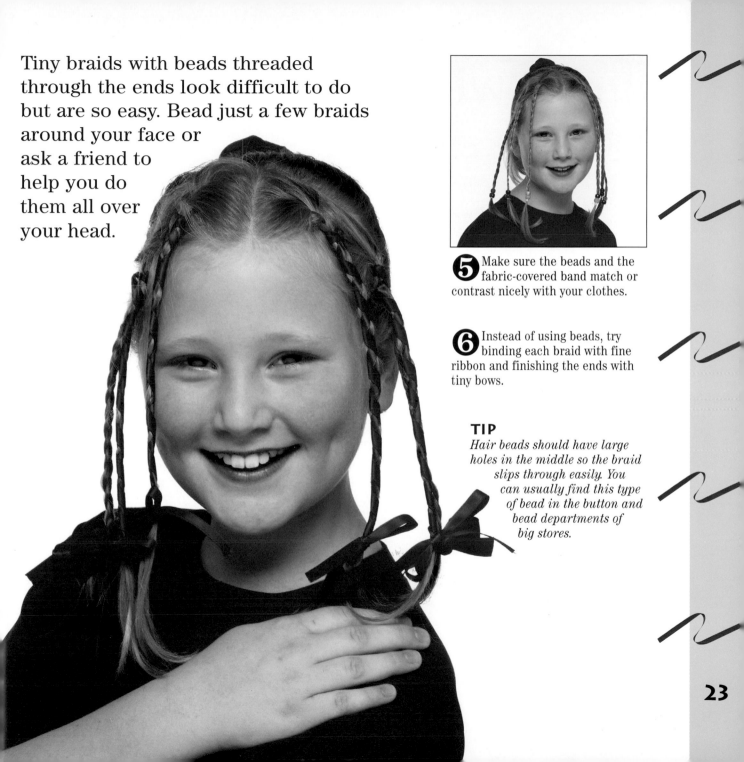

**5** Make sure the beads and the fabric-covered band match or contrast nicely with your clothes.

**6** Instead of using beads, try binding each braid with fine ribbon and finishing the ends with tiny bows.

**TIP**
*Hair beads should have large holes in the middle so the braid slips through easily. You can usually find this type of bead in the button and bead departments of big stores.*

# Tiny Twists

Finely braided hair need not look the same every day. It can be twisted into tiny coils and brightened up with covered bands.

**TIP**

*Fine braids like these can be left in the hair for weeks but it is best to remove hair accessories at night so that they don't pull your hair or get tangled up.*

**1** Take about six fine braids in one hand and twist them together. You will find that the hair starts to roll back on itself and begins to form a coil.

**2** Continue twisting, allowing the hair to coil around the finger of your other hand then carefully tuck the ends of the braids in, so the hair feels secure.

**3** Push a small covered band over the first two fingers of one hand and use the other hand to hold the coil of hair. Carefully slip the band over your hair and push it down so the braids are held tight.

**4** Make as many more twists as you want. We did four at the front and one in the middle of the back, but if you would like more simply use less hair for each one.

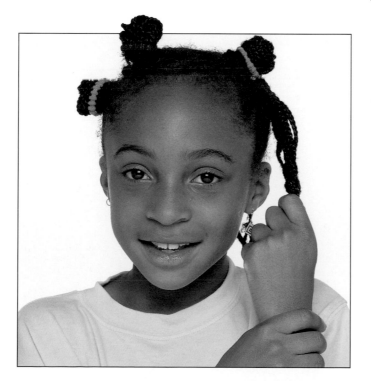

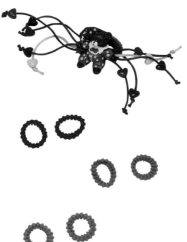

# Racy Ribbons

Braids look really good if you include ribbons as you go. At the ends tie each ribbon into a bow to make beautiful cascades of shades.

**TIP**
*Cut ends of ribbons on a slant to stop them fraying.*

**1** Part your hair in the middle and brush it through. Gather up the hair at each side and use a covered band to secure in bunches. Make the bunches at about ear level.

**2** Take three lengths of ribbon, each of a different shade. Pull the ends halfway through the band, then tie them onto it once. Make sure the ends are roughly even.

**3** Divide the hair into three strands and put two matching pieces of ribbon with each one. Now begin braiding as normal right down to the ends.

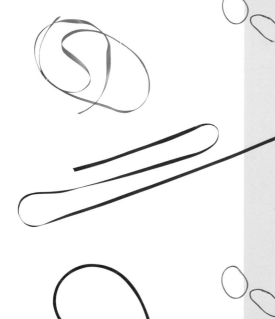

**4** Secure the end of the braid, including the ribbons, in a covered band. Now take each pair of matching ribbons and tie them in a bow. Braid and tie the other side.

**5** You could always put on a matching hairband and add a bow at the top of each braid.

# Braids and Bows

Simple braids can be used in many different ways. See how two can be tied at the back of the head in a pretty bow, while tiny front braids can be decorated with a few small beads.

**TIP**

*You could make a beaded band yourself. Thread beads onto lots of tiny lengths of cord and then tie them around a covered band. The more different shades you use, the better!*

**1** Part your hair in the middle, then take a small section of hair from one side. Start braiding near the roots and work all the way down to the ends. See page 6 for full details on how to braid.

**2** Take a small section of hair from the other side of your head and braid in exactly the same way. Secure the ends in a covered band, twisting and wrapping the band around until it holds tight.

**3** Take the braids around to the middle of the back of your head. Tie them together with a small piece of ribbon and loop it into a bow.

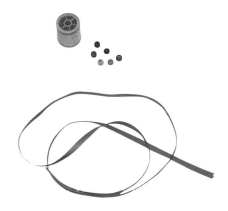

**4** Braid two more sections of hair, so that each one hangs in front of your ear. Thread three different shades of bead onto each braid. (See pages 10–11 for details.) It looks nice if at least one of the beads matches your ribbon bow.

**5** Finally, brush your hair (taking care not to spoil the braid or the bow) for a sleek finished look.

# Banded Bunches

Keep your bunches tidy by wrapping bright bands around them all the way to the bottom.

**TIP**

*Design your own motif bands by sewing novelty buttons onto small stretch bands.*

**1** Part your hair in the middle from front to back. Put a covered band over one hand so it sits on your knuckles, then slip it over this section of hair. Twist it back over until it's tight. Repeat for the other bunch.

**2** Take two small stretch bands (we used ones with little piggies on) and slip one over each bunch. You may need to twist them twice so they hold nicely.

**3** Take two more stretch bands in a different shade and slip a bunch through each band, about 5cm/2in from the first band.

**4** Take more stretch bands in different shades and continue adding them to your bunches, always about 5cm/2in from the last, until you run out of hair, or bands!

**5** Make sure the bands are at the same level all the way down both bunches. Why not clip pretty slides into the hair above each bunch?

# Pretty Ponytail

**1** Tip your head forwards and brush your hair from the back of your neck right to the ends. Make sure there are no tangles or knots. It is easiest if you use a brush with wide spaces between the bristles.

**2** Take hold of your hair with one hand and run the fingers of your other hand through your hair to make sure it is smooth. Keep hold of your hair and lift your head up.

**3** Put a fabric-covered band over the knuckles of one hand, then pull your hair though the band. Twist the band and pull your hair through again until tight enough.

**4** Add two more fabric-covered bands above the first one so that you get lots of height.

**5** Use covered bands in alternating shades, as it looks good if they cross over and form a pattern. Pin little net flowers in place with grips to add an extra splash of interest.

A really high ponytail, right on the top of your head, makes you instantly taller and is one of the easier styles to do.

**TIP**

*You can get fabric flowers in the sewing departments of large stores. Push a grip into the back of each flower to help you to fasten the flowers into your hair.*

# Ribbon Roll

**1** Use a comb with widely spaced teeth to help you smooth your hair up onto the top of your head. Hold your hair with one hand and put a covered band over the other hand. Twist the band around your hair to make a ponytail.

It's easy to make very curly hair look neat and tidy if you braid a high ponytail with ribbon and twirl it into a roll.

**2** Braid the ponytail from the top right down to the ends and secure the ends with another covered band. You could leave your hair just like this if you wanted to.

**3** Take a length of the ribbon and slip one end under the covered band at the top of your head and pull through, so the ends are even. Bind the ponytail with the ribbon right down to the ends.

**4** Take the ends of the ribbon and braid in one hand and roll the lot around on itself to make a bun. Use one or two grips to secure it in place but allow the ends of the ribbon to fall free.

**5** We added a dark blue, pale blue and white cord hairband to change the look into one ideal for parties. A hairband is useful for keeping your hair off your face.

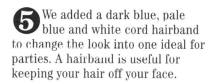

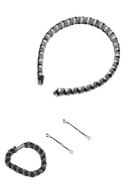

# Triple Twist

① Brush your hair into a low ponytail at the nape of your neck. Make sure the front is really smooth with no ends sticking out.

This is a perfect style if your hair is thick and wavy. The hair is divided into three and braided, then the three braids are formed into one. It looks complicated but is so easy to do.

**TIP**

*Look in your mother's sewing box for oddments of fabric and ask her to help you make your own fabric bands.*

**2** Divide the ponytail into three equal sections. Take the first one and braid it from top to bottom. Look again at the instructions on page 6 if you can't quite remember how to braid.

**3** When you get to the end of the braid, secure it with a covered band. Braid the other two sections in exactly the same way. You now have three braids to work with.

**4** Take the three single braids and braid them together in the same way as before. Your hair will form into a thick braid that looks like a twist of hair.

**5** Simply twist a covered band to hold the hair in one place. Alternatively, add two patterned chiffon hair accessories to each end of the twist for a different look.

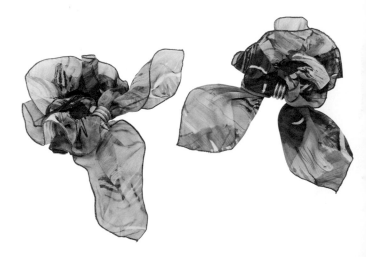

**37**

# Pony Princess

Here the top section of your hair is smoothed back and the rest of the hair held by cute stretch bands to make a two-toned ponytail.

**1** Brush your hair so there are no tangles or knots. Then use your thumbs to divide off the top section of your hair. Hold this section tightly with one hand.

**2** Use a small stretch band to secure this top section of hair. You may need to twist once or twice so the band is tight enough to hold the hair properly.

**3** Gather all your hair together at the nape of your neck and secure it in another small stretch band in a different shade. You may need to twist it again so it's tight enough to stay in place.

**TIP**

*Covered bands like these are made from flexible wire sewn into the edge of a long strip of fabric.*

38

**4** Take another stretch band and do the same thing again. The bands should sit neatly next to one another, so push them together.

**5** Add another stretch band further down the ponytail. Or take a bendy fabric band, place it around the back of your head and bring the ends up on top in the front. Twist the ends into a circle to hold the band in place.

39

# Be-Bop Bunches

High bunches like these are really easy to do on bob-length hair, and you can twist a section with ribbon for a really grown-up look too.

**1** Part your hair in the middle and brush your hair so it is really smooth. Take a small section at one side and brush again. You can experiment to see how large a section you'd like to use.

**TIP**
*To make your hair shiny always use cool water for the final rinse after you shampoo your hair.*

**2** Tie this small piece of hair in a band. We used crocheted silky bands in many shades, which look really good.

**3** Twist the band until it is tight enough to hold the hair in place. Repeat for the other side.

**4** Divide off a small section of the hair from one of the bunches and slip the end of the ribbon halfway through the covered band. Twist the ribbon around your hair and tie the ends in a bow.

**5** For that extra-special look, push grips through tiny fabric flowers of matching shades and use them as pretty accessories near one of the bunches.

# Bobbie Braids

**1** Divide the top section of your hair into two sets of braids. Take one section in one hand and slip a band over the other hand. You can use a plain band or one with beads attached to it.

**2** Slip the band over the braids, twist it around and slip the braids through the band again until it is tight enough to hold. Try to position the beads so that they are at the front.

**3** Take another band and tie it around the ends of the braids, twisting around and around until it is tight enough to hold. Again, position the beads so they are at the front. Repeat with the other side.

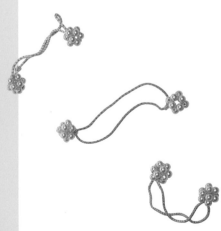

**4** Take all the back braids in one hand and slip over another covered band close to the back of your head to make a ponytail.

## TIP

*You can make beaded bands like the ones we used by threading about eight beads onto shirring (thin) elastic and tying them onto plain bands.*

Braiding hair all over the head is a traditional and practical way to keep it neat and tidy. Adding pretty accessories lets you ring the changes each day.

**5** Tie the end of the ponytail in a matching band to form a little tail.

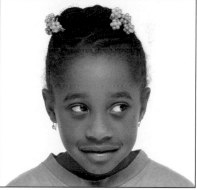

**6** Twist both the side ponytails into each other over the top of your head.

# Mini Ha Ha

**1** Part the hair in the middle and split off a section on one side. Braid as described on page 6 and then secure the ends in a covered band.

Mid-length hair can be triple-braided and then bound at the ends with bright bands.

**TIP**

*If you find that your hair is flyaway, ask your mother if you can borrow a silk scarf. Use the scarf to cover a bristle brush and stroke it over your hair. The static electricity, which makes hair wispy, magically disappears.*

44

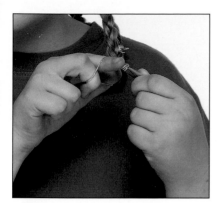

**2** Make five more braids in exactly the same way. There should be one either side at the front, two behind your ears and two at the back.

**3** Gather three braids together at one side and then braid these from roots to ends. It will be bulky to work with but still easy to do. Secure with a covered band.

**4** Repeat for the other side, working as before. Secure with a covered band, pushing it up a little way so it covers the previous bands and makes it look as if the braids have been bound.

**5** You can also add a hairband and bind the braids with fine matching or contrasting ribbon, finishing off with a bow.

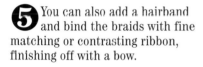

# Clever Cornrows

Cornrow braids look brilliant in bunches and are ideal for beading and adding bows.

**TIP**
*When washing cornrow-braided hair, rinse it thoroughly after shampooing to remove all the suds. This prevents the scalp getting dry, and feeling itchy and uncomfortable.*

**1** Braid tiny sections of hair working flat to the head. You will need some help to do the back and sides. Be patient as it will take some time.

**2** Divide the crown hair into two equal bundles of braids. Take one bundle in your hand and secure in a covered band, then repeat for the other side.

**3** Gather up all the braids at the back into one hand. Take a covered band and slip it over, twist the band and repeat until it is tight enough to hold the ponytail.

**4** You can add two beads to each braid, or just on some. If you want instructions on how to do this, see pages 10–11. You could use lots of different beads on each braid or choose them to match your clothes.

**5** You can also add tiny bows to the tops and bottoms of the bunches of braids. Use lots of thin, bright ribbons for this.

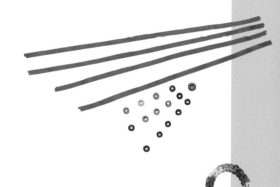

# Top and Tail

A simple braid takes on a party look if it is topped and tailed with fabric bands.

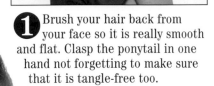

**1** Brush your hair back from your face so it is really smooth and flat. Clasp the ponytail in one hand not forgetting to make sure that it is tangle-free too.

**TIP**
*If you find you have lots of little pieces of hair sticking out, simply wet your hands and smooth over your hair to lay them flat.*

❷ Take a fabric-covered band and push it over one hand so it rests on your knuckles. Pass the ponytail through the fabric band, twist and turn until it is tight enough to hold your hair firmly.

❸ Divide the ponytail into three equal sections and braid it from the top to the bottom. Work right down until you are 5cm/2in from the bottom.

❹ Take a matching fabric-covered band and use it to secure the end of the braid. You may have to twist it up to three times to make sure it is tight enough.

❺ The result is a decorative and neat braid. For a more grown-up look, twist the braid around into a bun and secure it with a covered band. Add three grips decorated with rosebuds in a shade to match.

# Tufty Topknot

This fun style is really easy to do and is ideal for cornrow-braided hair.

**1** Scoop all the front braids together and hold them in place with one hand. Take a covered band in the other hand then slip it onto the braids. Twist to secure.

**2** Divide the bunch of braids into three equal sections and twist each set together to form a tuft of braids. Twist the ends together.

**3** Gather all the back braids together and secure them in a covered band. Try to do this in the middle of the back of your head so it looks neat.

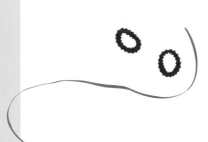

**TIP**

*If you have a plain bow you can make it extra special by sewing on some unusual beads or buttons. Ask your mother if you can look in her button box for something suitable.*

**4** Clip a large, floppy bow to the topknot. You can secure it through the covered band if you wish. Make sure the bow is right in the middle.

**5** For a party look, tie a small length of ribbon into a bow around the topknot and at the end of each tuft. Curl tiny lengths of paper ribbon (scrape your thumbnail along each one) then attach to grips and fasten them in your hair.

**51**

# Wonder Waves

Straight hair can be changed into a mass of waves by using fabric curlers, but you do need to leave them in overnight to get the best result.

**1** Take a fabric curler and fold it in half to grip a section of hair between the two pieces. Pull the curler right down to the bottom of the hair.

**2** Wind the fabric curler up the hair from the ends towards your head. Do this slowly and make sure you don't let go of either end of the curler.

**3** When you can wind no further, take the ends of the fabric curler and bring them both together, then cross them over. This is so that they hold the hair in place.

**4** Repeat all over your head. Remember, the bigger the sections of hair you wind, the looser the wave will be. For really tight curls, take only small sections and use lots of curlers.

**5** Leave your curlers in overnight. They are very soft so they won't keep you awake!

**6** In the morning remove each curler and use your fingers to 'rake' through each wave. You could also scoop the front hair back and secure it with a sunflower slide.

### TIP
*You will get an even curlier effect if your hair is just very slightly damp. But remember never to go to bed with wet hair.*

# Teeny Bopper

**1** Lift a section of hair from the front to the top of your head and then use a bristle brush to smooth the front of your hair. Do not brush through the length of your hair or you will pull the waves out.

**2** Take a large covered band (one that will wrap around lots of times) and use it to secure the top hair. Make sure you do this right in the middle, because you don't want your topknot to be lopsided.

**3** Take a section of hair at one side and fasten it with another large covered band in a different shade. Loosen the waves with your fingers, but don't brush or comb the length of your hair.

**4** Do exactly the same on the other side using another covered band in a different shade. You can, if you like, secure more bands like this at the crown.

Once you have waved your hair, you can create lots of other looks. Here, a trio of bands tames the waves and gives a fresh new style.

**TIP**

*If you want to keep your waves for as long as possible, only rake through them with your fingers or use a wide-toothed comb.*

# Braided and Bound

Long straight hair can be braided then wrapped with ribbons in different shades for a really snazzy style.

1 Take small sections of hair and braid them tightly from root to tip. See page 6 for full instructions on how to braid. You may need a friend to help you to braid the hair at the back.

2 Secure the end of each braid by wrapping with fine thread. Wrap it around a couple of times before tying into a tight knot. Snip off any long ends, but be careful not to cut your hair.

3 Take a piece of narrow ribbon and fold it in half. Tie the ribbon to the top of the braid, then bind downwards by crossing the ribbon over and over, first at the front of the braid, then at the back.

4 Continue binding until you reach the end of the braid and tie the ends of the ribbon. Repeat until you have bound all your braids. You may need a helping hand to do the braids at the back.

5 Scoop up the braids on the top of your head and bind them into a topknot with narrow ribbon.

### TIP

*Fine ribbons can be left in your hair overnight because they are soft and won't pull your hair.*

57

# Crimping Crazy

**1** Divide your hair into fine sections and braid it from the roots to the ends making the braids even and quite tight. The smaller the sections are, the finer the finished crimp will be.

**2** Secure the end of each braid with a piece of thread, wrap it around two or three times and then tie the ends into a little knot. If you prefer, you can use very small covered bands.

**3** Leave the braids overnight to set your hair into its new shape. You can lightly mist your hair with water if you wish but don't go to bed with wet hair.

**4** In the morning carefully unravel each braid, loosening it with your fingers as you go.

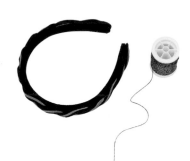

**TIP**
*Crimps will stay in your hair until you next wash it.*

Big girls use crimping irons to create ripples in their hair but you can get the same effect by braiding your hair and leaving it overnight to set.

**5** You can, if you wish, gently comb through using a wide-toothed comb or a brush with widely spaced teeth.

**6** Keep your hair away from your face using an attractive hairband.

# Double Dazzle

Once you have crimped your hair you can create different styles with it.

**1** Gently brush through your hair, but don't tug or pull it too much or you will loosen the crimps. Divide off a section of your hair at the front and hold it tightly in one hand.

**TIP**

*Paper flowers which are used to decorate presents make perfect hair accessories. You can find them in stationery shops or large stores.*

**2** Take a covered band and place it over the knuckles of the other hand. This makes it easier to secure the bunch. Do not let go and keep the bunch tight to your head.

**3** Pull your hair through the band, then twist the band and pull the hair through it again. Repeat until it is tight enough to hold the hair in place. Push the band close to the top of the bunch.

**4** Repeat for the other side, making another bunch in exactly the same way. Try to make sure you use about the same amount of hair in each bunch.

**5** Smooth the bunches down with your hands or a soft brush, but don't brush too hard! You could also take another section of hair on your crown and fix it in a covered band.

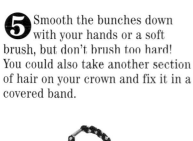

**61**

# Braided Flips

Braids can be bound tightly with cord for a really unusual style.

**1** Part your hair in the middle, and then braid the hair on one side from the roots to the ends. Keep the tension even so that your braid is straight.

**TIP**

*To bind braids, choose cord that is not too shiny, so that it doesn't slip off the braid.*

**2** Secure the end of the braid in a covered band, twisting it back until it is tight enough to hold. Repeat, making a braid in exactly the same way for the other side.

**3** Take a piece of fine cord and, starting at the top, bind the braid by wrapping the cord around and around it. Keep the circles of cord close to one another.

**4** Half way down your braid, you can change to a second cord in a different shade. Hold the ends of the first and second cords against your braid and bind the second cord tightly around the ends. Continue working all the way down to the end of your braid, and secure the end of the cord by tucking it into the covered band.

**5** Add two flowers or matching slides to either side of your head, either at the front or above the braids.

## ACKNOWLEDGEMENTS

*The publishers would like to thank the following girls for appearing in this book:*

Lauren Andrews, Charley Crittenden, Kimberley Durrance, Terri Ferguson, Sophia Groome, Nicola Kreinczes, Elouisa Markham, Tania Murphy, Lucy Oliver, Kim Peterson, Alexandra Richards, Leigh Richards, Kate Yudt.

*The publishers would also like to thank the following for lending hair accessories, brushes, combs and other equipment:*
Boots; Head Gardener, Knightsbridge; Lady Jayne; Mason Pearson, Kent; Molton Brown; Tesco.

This book is designed for children between the ages of 7 and 11. All beads, bows, threads and hair accessories should be kept out of reach of babies and small children.